AF379206

An Almost Human Gesture

An Almost Human Gesture

Louis Jenkins

co-published by

Eighties Press and Ally Press

Grateful acknowledgement is made to the editors of the following publications in which certain of these poems first appeared: *American Poetry Review, Appalachian Journal, Ascent, Barnwood, Bloomsbury Review, Carleton Miscellany, Chariton Review, Crazy Horse, Epoch, The Great Circumpolar Bear Cult, Hawaii Review, Indiana Review, Lake Superior Journal, Madrona, North Stone Review, Paris Review, Poetry East, Poetry Now, Port Cities, Puerto Del Sol,* and *Seneca Review.* Several of these poems were included in *Heartland II: Poets of the Midwest,* Lucian Stryk, ed. (Northern Illinois University Press); *Seven Lake Superior Poets,* David Kubach and Rick Penn, ed. (Bear Cult Press). The poems "Library" and "Violence on Television" appeared in *News Of The Universe,* Robert Bly, ed. (Sierra Club Books). Some of these poems were part of a selection of twenty-five prose poems by Louis Jenkins , published in *Poetry East,* No. 8.

Thanks to the Bush Foundation for grants which helped make possible the writing of some of these poems.

Cover illustration: "Two Human Beings. The Lonely Ones", by Edvard Munch. Acknowledgement to The City of Oslo Art Collections, The Munch Museum, Oslo, Norway.

Library of Congress Cataloging-in-Publication Data
Jenkins, Louis, 1942–
    An almost human gesture.

    I. Title.
PS3560.E488A78 1987   811'.54   87-30850
ISBN 0-915408-32-5

EIGHTIES PRESS & ALLY PRESS
Saint Paul • Minnesota

Table of Contents

THE ORDINARY AND THE EXTRAORDINARY

Louis Jenkins' poems seem at first to be ordinary details of familiar life laid out in familiar rhythms and everyday language. But reading carefully we discover extraordinary works of human memory. The poet may put his attention on the moment when the drunk gets up and finds the car gone, the summer in which the well digger's wife decides to live alone, or a fisherman's whole life; and the memory chooses out of millions of possible details eight or ten or twelve, seemingly — because the mood of his language does not insist on revelation — chosen randomly, haphazardly, off-handedly. Each memory appears straight-faced, as if to say, "This is nothing out of the ordinary." But when we've finished a poem, we feel astonished as we study it, and see that each detail the memory called up fits into some invisible whole, and, once present, locks into a steely pattern. The "facts" are so integrated now that no detail can fall away even if we shake the poem.

A fat teaching assistant has caught a freshman cheating on his exam and she stands now in the hallway displaying the evidence, telling the story to her colleagues: "I could tell by the way he looked. I could tell by his hands." With each detail the story expands, rooms are added, hallways, chandeliers, flights of stairs, and she sinks exhausted against a railing. More listeners arrive and she begins again. She seems thinner now, lighter. She rises, turns. She

Who can say why these particular details make a
psychic whole around a moment of guilt and punishment?
The accuracy leads to disturbance. Fancy, in the dis-
tinction Coleridge insists on, leads to a charming surface,
which assures us all is well; but imagination is open to
distant trouble, and makes the soul feel as if it is, in
Holderlin's clause, swaying, "as in a rocking boat on the
sea."

I feel that two people are talking in Louis Jenkins'
poems, though neither identifies himself. A forceful child,
powerful, magical and sometimes angry encounters the
adult form of himself. The child is often enraged, and takes
the form of a motorcycle that will not start, a messenger
whose job is to carry an egg over dangerous roads to the
Czar, a psychic who can walk through solid walls, a
fisherman looking for a quiet place to live. If he finds the
quiet place, the adult will begin immediately to film it. The
interior child wants isolation, and sometimes, disguised
perhaps as a well digger's wife, achieves it. "The sound of
boots slogging through the mud is gone and the rocks roll
away miles below me." The adult wants mail, but the child
as mail carrier refuses to deliver the mail and longs to be
the Greek runner sent to report the Persian battle who
collapses in Athens gasping, "No news." In this bitter
battle between child and adult he is one of the inheritors of
James Wright.

A droll humor colors all the poems, and it comes from
the incongruity of the child's grief and the adult's cliche.

" 'It's no use,' he says, 'she's left me.' It's as if he had said 'Van Gogh is my favorite painter.' "

It is neither the child nor the adult, but the poet who chooses with such apparent casualness the resonant details. Louis Jenkins finds himself in the boat of imagination, which carries him into an underground river, which puts him in touch with depth, the mysterious unities far below consciousness, the joined opposites of child and adult, courage and cowardice, activity and inertness. We feel troubled, and don't always know where we are. A new mother is sure that the first baby brought to her was a girl and not the son later brought in. "They said there was only one baby born, a boy. I'm certain now there were two. I know the little girl is alive somewhere but I have no idea how to find her. . ."

I'm delighted to welcome Louis Jenkins' first full-length book of poems. Its appearance at this moment seems appropriate to our national life. During the sixties the United States was a hawk attacking mice with its beak. Now it acts like a blinded owl. Like other poets in his generation, Charles Simic, Gerald Stern, and Russell Edson, Louis Jenkins calls attention to what the nation cannot see, cannot welcome, the children it cannot care for. "By midnight the crew is drunk and the ship is dead in the water. The captain is furious and shouts over the intercom to the engine room. But they are all asleep, rocked in their little cradle on the sea."

Robert Bly

For Ann and Lars

BASKETBALL

A huge summer afternoon with no sign of rain . . . elm trees
in the farmyard bend and creak in the wind. The leaves are
dry and gray. In the driveway a boy shoots a basketball at a
goal above the garage door. Wind makes shooting difficult
and time after time he chases the loose ball. He shoots,
rebounds, turns, shoots . . . on into the afternoon. In the
silence between the gusts of wind the only sounds are the
thump of the ball on the ground and the rattle of the bare
steel rim of the goal. The gate bangs in the wind, the dog in
the yard yawns, stretches and goes back to sleep. A film of
dust covers the water in the trough. Great clouds of dust
rise from open fields that stretch a thousand miles beyond
the horizon.

LIFE IS SO COMPLEX

Life is so complex, even though you eat brown rice and brush your teeth with baking soda. Simplify. Spend the day alone. Spend it fishing. Watch the line and the motion of the water; your thoughts drift. . . a slight bump and a steady pull on the line and the whole line of cars begins to move as the train pulls out of the station. Someone takes the seat beside you, someone at the end of a love affair. The threats of murder and suicide, the pleading, the practical jokes, became at the end only tiresome and she is relieved at his going. She turns away before the train is out of sight.

Your ordinary life is simple, full of promise, bullet-like, pushing aside the waves of air, moving with incredible speed toward the life that waits, motionless, unsuspecting, at the heart of the forest.

A QUIET PLACE

I have come to understand my love for you. I came to you like a man, world-weary, looking for a quiet place. The gas station and grocery store, the church, the abandoned school, a few old houses, the river with its cool shady spots. . . good fishing. How I've longed for a place like this! As soon as I got here I knew I'd found it. Tomorrow the set production and camera crews arrive. We can begin filming on Monday: the story of a man looking for a quiet place.

THE UKRAINIAN EASTER EGG

It is quite different from the ordinary Ukrainian Easter Egg because of the pictures. On one side the sun setting over Los Angeles and opposite, soldiers sitting in the muddy trenches. They look cold, smoking cigarettes. Here is the violin hidden in the soup kettle and there is a family of cats living in an abandoned gas station. There are so many pictures: the barbed wire and the road through the forest, the ducks, the radio, the yellow, smoky fires along the railroad track where the lovers are taking a walk. In the morning the elders of the village decide what must be done. A brave man must ride the fastest horse and deliver the egg. The journey is long, the roads are dangerous. The egg must be given only to the Czar.

FIRST SNOW

By dusk the snow is already partially melted. There are dark patches where the grass shows through, like islands in the sea seen from an airplane. Which one is home? The one I left as a child? They all seem the same now. What became of my parents? What about all those things I started and never finished? What were they? As we get older we become more alone. The man and his wife share this gift. It is their breakfast: coffee and silence, morning sunlight. They make love or they quarrel. They move through the day, she on the black squares, he on the white. At night they sit by the fire, he reading his book, she knitting. The fire is agitated. The wind hoots in the chimney like a child blowing in a bottle, happily.

FOOTBALL

I take the snap from center, fake to the right, fade back . . .
I've got protection. I've got a receiver open downfield . . . .
What the hell is this? This isn't a football it's a shoe. A man's
brown leather oxford. A cousin to a football, maybe, the
same skin, but not the same, a thing made for the earth, not
the air. I realize that this is a world where anything is
possible and I understand, also, that one often has to make
do with what one has. I have eaten pancakes, for instance,
with that clear corn syrup on them because there was no
maple syrup and they weren't very good. Well, anyway, this
is different. (My man downfield is waving his arms.) One
has certain responsibilities, one has to make choices. This
isn't right and I'm not going to throw it.

MEDICINE

He sits in a chair and does not move for a long time. He thinks he should do something, take some action, but he doesn't know what. Nothing seems worth the effort. He leans his head back to rest against the wall, stretches out his legs and is still again. The way he sits he seems a part of something else, one side of a mountain perhaps, the way it slopes down to flat land. This year the crops burned up, livestock died. The ground is cracked and dry. The little girl is sick. The wife hardly speaks and lies down each night beside the sick child. The farmer walks out to look at the sky, hands at his sides, followed by a skinny dog. It is nearly dark. The moon rises making a shadowy light on the trail. A man on horseback dressed in black is coming down the trail, the man from the medicine show, bringing his bottles down from the mountain. Bottles of pure water. With each careful step of the pony the bottles in the saddlebags clink together. The man is singing quietly to himself.

MOTORCYCLE

He climbs on, switches on the ignition, kicks the starter: once, twice, three, four, five times . . . nothing. He tries a dozen more times. It won't go. He checks the gas tank. Got gas. He switches the key off and on, tries again. It still won't go. He climbs off the bike and squats down to look at the engine. Check the carburetor, check the wires . . . seems okay. He takes a wrench from his jacket pocket and removes the spark plug. He examines it, blows on it, wipes it on his jeans, replaces the plug, climbs back on the bike and tries again. Nothing. Now he is getting really angry. There is absolutely no reason why this thing shouldn't start. He gets off the bike and stands and stares at it. He gets back on and kicks the starter really hard half-a-dozen times. Now he is furious. He gets off and throws the wrench he is still holding as far as he can. It bounces on the gravel down the road and skids into the weeds in the ditch. Then he turns and kicks the son-of-a-bitch motorcycle over on its side and walks away. After a short distance he thinks better of it and returns to the motorcycle. It isn't sobbing quietly. It doesn't say "I don't want to play with you any more" or "I don't love you any more" or "I have my own life to live" or "I have the children to think of." It only lies there leaking oil and gas. He rights the motorcycle and carefully wipes off the dust, carefully mounts and once more tries the starter. Even now it won't go. He gets down and sits in the dirt beside the broken motorcycle.

WAR SURPLUS

Aisle after aisle of canvas and khaki, helmets and mess kits, duffle bags, pea coats, gas masks . . . . Somewhere there is a whole field of abandoned aircraft, all kinds, P-38's, B-25's . . . . All you have to do is wait until dark, climb over the fence, pull the blocks from the wheels, climb in, start the engines and taxi out to the strip. It's easy. You can fly without ever having had a lesson.

A beautiful woman dressed in black sits on a bench near a grave. A tall man in dress uniform stands beside her and puts his hand on her shoulder. She says "I come here often; it is so peaceful." He says "Before John died, he asked me to look after you." They embrace. Behind them are many neat rows of white crosses extending over a green hill where the flag is flying proudly.

The engines make a deep drone, a comforting sound, and the light from the instrument panel tells you everything is stable and right. Below are silver-tufted clouds and tiny enemy towns, lovely toy towns, all lighted by the bombers' moon.

OCTOBER

October is the month of disappearance: geese flying overhead, an automobile abandoned by the roadside . . . . There is an uneasiness in the trees, low voices: *"Someone absolutely has to stay with Mother all the time. . . ." "No, he has very few visitors and no one has seen him or his dog for well over a week."* Someone forces the door and steps inside. . . .

The nights are cold, the days are bright and filled with pointless activity, such as raking leaves. Here in the woods no one rakes the leaves. Red and orange maple leaves fall first, then the yellow birch and poplar, one on another. If you clear away a few from that little pool, there is the perfect sky again on the other side, and a face, not quite your own, that apes your every move and will not go away until you do.

THE ICE FISHERMAN

From here he appears as a black spot, one of the shadows that today has found it necessary to assume solid form. Along with the black jut of shoreline far to the left, he is the only break in the undifferentiated gray of ice and overcast sky. Here is a man going jiggidy-jig-jig in a black hole. Depth and the current are of only incidental interest to him. He's after something big, something down there that is pure need, something that, had it the wherewithal, would swallow him whole. Right now nothing is happening. The fisherman stands and straightens, back to the wind. He stays out on the ice all day.

THE WELL DIGGER'S WIFE

I've been thinking of mountains on these hot nights, or better yet, the window ledge high above the bed and this tangle of sheets. It must be cool there with the breeze from the open window, and clean, painted white, like snow, only not so cold or wet. And not so steep as a mountain top, like a great plain stretching out for miles. I started to move there once, last summer, taking just a few things I'd need: the cat, the mirror, a hatful of needles. But then he came home and caught me, broke two of my ribs and put an ugly bruise on my cheek. Every day now the sound of digging grows more faint. The sound of boots slogging through the mud is gone and the rocks roll away miles below me.

MARGARET LUOMA

At her age a fall could have meant a serious injury, a
sprained ankle or a broken hip. Luckily there was only a
bruise and the terrible embarrassment. She pulled away
from the young man who helped her to her feet, said
"Thank you, I'm all right" and went on her way as quickly as
she could without looking back. But she couldn't forget
about it. His face. . . like a photograph on the piano,
thoughtful, always young. "All that concern," she thought.
"What did he care?" It began to seem as though he'd
caused the bruises, actually pushed her down. She didn't
need him. She was old now. A lifetime of love wasted.

SERGEANT NORQUIST

Two years ago I thought seriously about killing myself. I looked at guns in the pawn shops. Then, I don't know why exactly, I turned to God. I have my job at the paper mill and this room, but they mean nothing to me. My real life begins when I put on the uniform and make my rounds. I go to all the bars downtown, even the worst ones along First Street. I say "Good evening, Salvation Army" and people give me their change, good people mostly. Once in a while a guy will say "This ain't no church" or something like that, but no one has ever really given me a hard time. Most people respect the uniform. One evening in the *Oasis* a woman kissed me. I gave her a copy of the *War Cry*. She wasn't an old woman either, but she had lived hard. I still pray for her. A lot of people talk to me. They tell me their days are hard to get through and I know about that. At night sometimes, when I can't sleep, I think of all the money I've collected. I close my eyes and see all those nickels and dimes rising from the bars on First Street and from run-down places all over town, from poor people, like a reversed rain, from earth to heaven. I think nothing in heaven would grow if that rain didn't fall.

THE PLAGIARIST

A fat teaching assistant has caught a freshman cheating on his exam and she stands now in the hallway displaying the evidence, telling the story to her colleagues: "I could tell by the way he looked. I could tell by his hands." With each detail the story expands, rooms are added, hallways, chandeliers, flights of stairs, and she sinks exhausted against a railing. More listeners arrive and she begins again. She seems thinner now, lighter. She rises, turns. She seems almost to be dancing. She clutches the paper of the wretched student. He holds her firmly, gently as they turn and turn across the marble floor. The lords and ladies fall back to watch as they move toward the balcony and the summer night. Below in the courtyard soldiers assemble, their brass and steel shining in the moonlight.

THE HERMIT

It's true that the best part of a trip lies between the starting place and the destination. The fun is in the getting there. And it's not always what you see along the way but what you can't see, or can just barely see: the place where the spruce and hemlock fade into the mist and smoke rises from some hidden cabin. The man who has lived here twenty-five years, winter and summer, alone, comes out carrying a shotgun when you approach. Not unfriendly, just cautious. But he has nothing to hide. He talks about county taxes. He doesn't keep a dog. Dogs run the deer in the spring when there's a crust on the snow. It doesn't take a big dog to bring down a deer, either. He says he's shot maybe thirty, thirty-five dogs since he's lived here. As he talks, mosquitoes land on his face and neck but he doesn't bother to brush them away. Maybe he doesn't regret not wasting his youth in unrequited love. Probably he never thinks of it. Or if he does, only absently, the way you notice cars passing on the interstate a mile from here.

APPLEJACK

Wilma worked sixteen years for a plumbing and heating company and never married. She lived with her mother in a little house out in Arnold township. And her mother, who was crazy from drinking applejack, would hide behind the door when Wilma came home from work and try to stab her with a butcher knife. Wilma didn't know what to do. When she thought of having her put in a rest home, the old lady would cry and Wilma's aunt in Seattle would write letters saying "Don't you dare put my sister in a rest home." This went on for years and Wilma began drinking applejack too. When the old woman finally died, Wilma quit her job, lived alone in the house and wore her mother's clothes.

I know of a man killed driving his pickup a hundred miles an hour, and another who left his wife and family and ran off with a redheaded high school girl. They had been drinking applejack.

Now, when the birch and maple leaves have fallen and blow nervously around the roads, the juice from this year's apples has begun to ferment. This is no ordinary applejack. The bottles may remain hidden for years, deep down among the roots and the dead, before someone takes the first sip.

TWINS

The first baby they brought into my room was a girl. I held her for a few minutes then the nurse took her away. I never saw the baby again or the nurse who brought her. Later another nurse brought the boy, my son. When I told my husband he said it was probably just the effect of the anesthetic, but I made him check. They said there was only one baby born, a boy. I'm certain now there were two. I know the little girl is alive somewhere but I have no idea how to find her. I can only watch her brother for signs . . . you know, the way twins sense things about each other. Sometimes I'm afraid when he goes off to school, lost among so many other children. When he comes home in the afternoon I catch him and hold him a moment and look into his eyes before he pulls away to run outside and play with his friends. I can't really say what I'm looking for. I think I'll only know if something is missing, a certain look or a gesture . . . I think I'll know if that life dies out in him. I can't explain that to him, of course, or to his father; he would only say I've got too much imagination.

MARLENE NOLUND

She's packed the kids off to spend the weekend with their father. At last she has the place to herself, a rented farmhouse, a couple dozen chickens, a pickup that works part-time and a child-support check she finally managed to get from her ex-husband. His problem was that he didn't want anything much. He was happy being a bricklayer or being in the army, happy just hanging around the house. She puts on her best dress and stands in front of the mirror, brushing her hair. She looks good, a little big in the chest maybe, but good for being the mother of two. It's mid-afternoon and the whole weekend is ahead. The summer wind nags at the house and flaps the blind at the window behind her so that it sounds like someone impatiently turning the pages of a newspaper. She imagines a man there, lying on the bed, glancing up occasionally to hurry her along, jingling the change in his pocket. It makes her nervous and angry. She fidgets with the dress, extracts a pair of earrings from the clutter of perfume and baby bottles on the bureau, smears her makeup. She hurries. It isn't what she wants.

A NEW CAR

He comes in late Saturday night, drunk. She pretends to be asleep when he comes to bed. Long before he wakes, Sunday morning, she is up and dressed. She dresses the child and drives away into the early fog. She drives 80 mph over the blacktop country roads for several hours. When he wakes the sun is shining and the house is quiet. He has a hangover and thinks perhaps he has been robbed. He feels his pants pocket for his wallet. He stands at the window and looks out at the empty driveway. When she returns he is sitting at the kitchen table drinking coffee. "Where have you been?" he says. She says "I had to take the baby to Sunday School; I can't depend on you to do it." He returns to the window and looks at the car. It's getting worn out he thinks, needs brakes and tires. He wishes he could afford a new one.

THE BLIND MAN

He comes down the hill at a slight angle to the sidewalk, hesitantly, moving his red-tipped white cane from side to side until it touches the fender of a lavender Pontiac parked at the curb. Then he stops. He reaches out with his left hand until he touches the cold metal pole of a No Parking sign, pulls himself close, stands with his arm wrapped around the pole in the narrow space between pole and car, waits and listens. He seems unsure, seems to have difficulty sorting the various sounds. Traffic to the right, traffic behind, wind blowing uphill from the Lake, the sound of a few leaves on the concrete. No passersby. End of the day, end of fall. He listens, head slightly raised, hat pushed back, eyes closed. He is neither young nor old: a man between a car and a pole. He waits a long time. Then he moves his cane to the right, up into the rear wheelwell of the car, then away to the left. He releases the pole and takes two careful steps downhill, moving the cane in front of him.

PAAVO WIRKKILA

There is something about a clearing that makes me feel
uneasy, something too sunny and optimistic about this
break in the constant shade, those nervous poplars and
gloomy spruce all turned to face an open space as if they
expected something to happen here: the blank page on which
something must be written.

Paavo Wirkkila got an idea, cleared the land and grew hay.
Nothing else grows very well around here. He kept a horse
to help with the hay then fed the hay to the horse. A limited
plan. When the old man died he left the buildings to fall,
left the clearing to the county and sapling popple trees. He
also left this heap of stones he'd cleared from the field. Not
a monument, no part of his plan . . . . Just an annoyance he
tried to push out of his earthly way.

ASLEEP AT THE WHEEL

He falls asleep at the wheel and dreams that everything is the same; he is still driving at night through the long pine forest. Mile after mile glides through the automobile. He manages distances more easily now so there is time to discern in the night forest a single tree, a stone, or a hidden path. These things seem as familiar and absorbing as a love affair or his own childhood. He sees for the first time that the forest extends not fifty or a hundred miles, but infinitely on either side of the road, and that it is possible to wander there forever, alone, and not die . . . . The car veers into the gravel at the edge of the blacktop. He wrenches the wheel back to the left. He is wide awake. The car is on the road, speeding toward the end of its headlight beams.

APPOINTED ROUNDS

At first he refused to deliver junk mail because it was stupid, all those deodorant ads, money-making ideas and contests. Then he began to doubt the importance of the other mail he carried. He began to select first class mail randomly for non-delivery. After he had finished his mail route each day he would return home with his handful of letters and put them in the attic. He didn't open them and never even looked at them again. It was as if he were an agent of Fate, capricious and blind. In the several years before he was caught, friends vanished, marriages failed, business deals fell through. Toward the end he became more and more bold, deleting houses, then whole blocks, from his route. He began to feel he'd been born in the wrong era. If only he could have been a Pony Express rider galloping into some prairie town with an empty bag, or the runner from Marathon collapsing in the streets of Athens, gasping, "No news."

SAILORS

When the ship gets into port the sailors all go nuts. They get drunk and dance and wake up the next afternoon in the whorehouse. And if a sailor gets thrown in jail he doesn't care because he just got paid and has enough money to get out. None of the sailors wants to go back to the ship. One thing sailors can't stand is the sight of water. One sailor hides out in a laundromat. One makes plans to marry. Another is still drunk. The sailors hate this lousy port. The ship sails at dawn with all hands, but someone has sneaked whiskey aboard. By midnight the crew is drunk and the ship is dead in the water. The captain is furious and shouts over the intercom to the engine room. But they are all asleep, rocked in their little cradle on the sea.

FROST FLOWERS

In the morning people go off to work all wrapped and bundled, through frozen doors, over cracking snow, huffing and puffing, each fueled by some simmering private indignation: low pay, something that was said at break . . . .The sun is far away on the southern horizon, a vague hope, more distant than the Caribbean. Eight below zero at eleven o'clock. The coffee boils and grows bitter. All afternoon the same old thing, knucklebone of mastadon, stews on the stove. The radiator hisses at the long shadows which finally engulf the winter day. Lights come on for a time in the houses and go out one by one. We breathe deeply of the dark. We exhale great plumes and fronds that form on the windows. Intricate icy blossoms open around us all night.

INTERMISSION

The violins have gone, the brass and woodwinds have gone. The orchestra has just finished a Paganini concerto. The basses and cellos lie on the floor or recline against chairs, weary and unimpressed. They are like soldiers or prisoners on a ten-minute break and no one has any cigarettes. In a far corner, dressed in black, the percussionist hunches over the tympany like a raven picking over a rabbit killed on the highway or like an old woman bending over a kettle, brewing a poison to be painted on telephone poles to kill all the woodpeckers. He tunes and tests the drum. What does he hear? A distant storm? A herd of buffalo? Perhaps railroad crews working hard to lay down track a few miles ahead of a locomotive; the cars richly furnished with carpet, crystal and fine wine. The beautiful ladies and gentlemen come laughing and talking down the aisles to find their seats.

PALISADE HEAD

Two hundred feet straight down from here the water boils up on the shore, and farther out is translucent blue-green, rising in even swells. Twenty feet beneath the surface just the tops of big ugly boulders become visible: old men and women at the bottom of stairs whispering and grumbling forever. They save things. They tell drowned-sailor jokes. They spend all their lives down there with algae that need water and sunlight, nothing more. I don't know what we are in our most secret selves, but I don't believe it is the free animal we long to be, beautiful and cruel. It is something more simple and more incomprehensible. Looking over the edge makes me a little sick. On those darkest nights of rain and northeast wind, small stones slip away and are never missed. This is a place of lichen and stubborn trees, a place where only lovers should walk.

32 DEGREES F.

The thermometer says exactly 32 degrees, freezing or melting. Neither here nor there . . . at the border, in a room without enough chairs, waiting with your bundle of possessions and the uneasy feeling that none of these things will be adequate on the other side. Outside the window a single drop of water hangs on the tip of an icicle for hours. A long time ago she showed me how to take the blossom at the base, snap off the stem, then carefully withdraw the pistil, pulling it slowly down until the little globe of nectar poised there, ready to take on the tongue. The single drop distilled from a lifetime falls to shatter on the frozen ground and the mindless soul flies away to its heaven on the honeysuckle south wind, that's come five hundred miles over the snow.

THE LIGHTHOUSE

Light flashes across the water and is gone, like headlights across the wall of a dark room where someone is lying awake. It happens so quickly; no way to take back the things that were said. *Your* son drove headlong into a train. *Your* daughter is in a Mexican jail. It's a house passed at eighty miles an hour. Did anyone live there? The night, the sea, the wind and the rocks, the terrible current off shore. . . . It is good to see the light across the water. It is a warning. This is the place where the land ends and the water begins or the water ends and the land begins. Either way is dangerous.

THE WAY

Even if you believe in Jesus there comes a moment when everything sinks. It is that moment when the fire collapses in the grate and the skinny sticks lie there smouldering, broken like the bones of the saints. See, even though you have come only this far your Ever Ready batteries have begun to fail and it *is* a swamp . . . or say it's a city street, but the first person you meet is a small man wearing a straw hat and striped overalls that are clean and starched. His hands and feet are very small and only the tips of his shiny black shoes stick out from the big legs of his pants. He has something in his pocket that shines, a cross or a switchblade. He asks your name and says he knows some of your family. He's crazy. He shows you a dance in which the movements are something like those of a goose. It is called "The Dance of People Who Look Just Alike". He says he will tell you a story about a woman he knows who has lived for years above a grocery store. He knows her very well and will take you to meet her. Now you have lingered here so long it is growing dark. There is no one on the street. You will have to spend the night here and you had hoped to make it at least to Cincinnati.

TAMARACKS

In the evening I am drawn to the tamaracks that bend and straighten in the wind like oarsmen pulling the long boat. It is only the longing to be safely dead, the desire for peace. But perhaps, even in death you would be restless, driving the back roads, a pocket full of change for the telephone, calling across the country at a terrible hour. I think that ghosts are the insomniacs among the dead. The only dead man I ever talked to told me that there used to be a tennis court where my house is now. "That's right. I used to walk here in the evenings when I was a young man." I was impatient. I said "I want to hear what things are like for you now." He said "Oh, people always ask me that. Can you explain to a child what it's like to be grown up? It's the same thing. I can tell you this though: times change. I was a blacksmith but I had to get into small engine repair in order to stay in business." "Oh, crap!" I said, and he vanished. The tamaracks accept the darkness just as the little pools of water accept the last portion of light. The air takes the water, leaving the road clear and dry.

THE DUTCH SHOE

She was out of the water for years, since the early fifties maybe, over at the shipyard in Superior. You could see her from the highway, her masts down, sails stowed away. I loved that boat. All the time I was growing up I made plans to buy her someday. What shall I say happened? That my father bought her and put her in the back yard and kept garden tools in the hold? Or that my mother bought her and kept her in the china closet with the jade Buddha and the eight-day clock? That her brass gleams in the firelight, still dry and harmless? No. I bought the Dutch Shoe and sailed to Rangoon and Singapore and a hundred other places. I faced incredible dangers and hardships. I talk loud and drink all night. When I snore I wake bears in the forest and fish in the sea. Early mist rises. Ice forms on the masts. My hair has turned white and my teeth have fallen out. I can't see a thing and I am sailing away.

IN A TAVERN

"It's no use," he says, "she's left me." This is after several drinks. It's as if he had said "Van Gogh is my favorite painter." It's a dimestore print he has added to his collection. He's been waiting all evening to show it to me. He doesn't see it. To him it's an incredible landscape, empty, a desert. "My life is empty." He likes the simplicity. "My life is empty. She won't come back." It is a landmark, like the blue mountains in the distance that never change. The crust of sand gives way with each step, tiny lizards skitter out of the way . . . . Even after walking all day there is no change in the horizon. "We're lost," he says. "No," I say, "let's go on." He says, "You go on. Take my canteen. You've got a reason to live." "No," I say, "we're in this together and we'll both make it out of here."

THE LAKE

Streets run straight downhill to the water. The lake brings the city to an end. It is there, always, changing the direction of my walks. Sometimes I go for days without coming near, catching only a glimpse through the trees: a sail, a white speck turning on the dark blue. Perhaps someone very old touched the back of my wrist, lightly, for only the briefest moment, or you said something to me. What was it? The waters close above my head suddenly without a sound.

CONFESSIONAL POEM

I have this large tattoo on my chest. It is like a dream I have while I am awake. I see it in the mirror as I shave and brush my teeth, or when I change my shirt or make love. What can I do? I can't remember where I got the tattoo. When in the past did I live such a life? And the price of having such a large tattoo removed must be completely beyond reason. Still, the workmanship of the drawing is excellent, a landscape 8x10 inches in full color, showing cattle going downhill into a small western town. A young man, who might have been my great-grandfather, dressed as a cowboy and holding a rifle, stands at the top of the hill and points down toward the town. The caption beneath the picture reads: "Gosh, I didn't know we were this far west."

THE HOUSE AT THE LAKE

This house is nearly a hundred years old. Some of the trees around it are even older, tall pines and spruce that shade the many rooms. In this room Great-Grandpa Torgeson spent the last ten years of his life and wouldn't talk to anyone. Grandma knows the story. The kitchen has been remodeled, and the bathrooms. The rest of the house is the same as when it was built. Most of the year the house is empty, but everyone vacations here. The family has gotten quite large with Duane and Kathy and their kids and Eileen and her kids and Judy and Art. The children spend the morning wading in the sunny shallows of the lake. Little fish, chubs and shiners, small perch and sunfish nibble at their toes and find food in the sand stirred up from the bottom. Inside the house the talk is usually business, stocks and family property. The children splash and laugh and squeal until someone from the house calls "Come in children." It's a voice that carries across the deep water of the lake where big muskies with their many rows of teeth glide through whatever grows or was lost down there . . . . *Come in. Time for lunch. Time for sleep.*

LIBRARY

I sit down at a table and open a book of poems and move slowly into the shadow of tall trees. They are white pines, I think. The ground is covered with soft brown needles and there are signs that animals have come here silently and vanished before I could catch sight of them. But here the trail edges into a cedar swamp: wet ground, deadfall and rotting leaves. I move carefully but rapidly, pleased with myself. Someone else comes and sits down at the table, a serious-looking young man with a large stack of books. He takes a book from the top of the stack and opens it. The book is called *How to Get a High-Paying Job*. He flips through it and lays it down and picks up another and pages through it quickly. It is titled *Moving Ahead*. We are moving ahead more rapidly now, through a second growth of popple and birch, our faces scratched and our clothes torn by the underbrush. We are moving even faster, marking the trail, followed closely by bulldozers and crews from the paper company.

THE FLOOD

Every so often, a girl calls me on the phone and tells me that she loves me, can't live without me, etc. The first time she called I was intrigued and flattered, naturally. But when I asked her name she ignored me and went right on talking. "Could we meet somewhere?" Again she ignored the question. Finally I became irritated and hung up. Obviously it was some kind of joke. She called several more times over the next few months and each time the result was the same. "What's the point?" I ask. "I love you," she says. A few weeks ago the bridge on 21st Street washed out. People came from all over town to help with the work and to watch the river overflow its banks and pour through the streets, the first flood in many years. Men were hard at work piling up sandbags to hold back the water. Near where I was standing, a pay telephone kept ringing and ringing. Finally, since no one else did, I answered. I thought perhaps it was someone calling with instructions for the flood control workers, but no. It was a man having trouble with his refrigerator. I guess he thought I was a repairman. No sooner had he hung up than the phone rang again: a woman looking for her child. No, I hadn't seen him. Call after call came in. It was as if people were actually telephoning the flood. For some reason I kept answering the phone. Then she called. "Hello," a pause. "Hello," I said again. "Louis," she said, "Louis—is that you?" I hung up the phone and stepped out of the booth. It was a relief to be in the open air again. I stood a moment looking at the muddy water while the phone continued to ring.

INVISIBLE

There are moments when a person cannot be seen by the human eye. I'm sure you've noticed this. You might be walking down the street or sitting in a chair when someone you know very well, your mother or your best friend, walks past without seeing you. Later they'll say "Oh, I must have been preoccupied." Not so. At times we are caught in a warp of space or time and, for a moment, vanish. This phenomenon occurs often among children and old people. No one understands exactly how this happens but some people remain invisible for long periods of time. Most of these do so by choice. They have learned to ride the moment, as a surfer rides the long curl of a wave. How exhilarating it is to ride like that: a feeling of triumph to move from room to room unseen, with only the slightest breeze from your passing.

VIOLENCE ON TELEVISION

It is best to turn on the set only after all the stations have gone off the air and just watch the snowfall. This is the other life you have been promising yourself: somewhere back in the woods, ten miles from the nearest town, and that just a wide place in the road with a tavern and a gas station. When you drive home, after midnight, half drunk, the roads are treacherous. And your wife is home alone, worried, looking anxiously out at the snow. This snow has been falling steadily for days, so steadily the snow plows can't keep up. So you drive slowly, peering down the road. And there! Did you see it? Just at the edge of your headlight beams, something, a large animal, or a man, crossed the road. Stop. There he is among the birches, a tall man wearing a white suit. No, it isn't a man. Whatever it is, it motions to you, an almost human gesture, then retreats farther into the woods. He stops and motions again. The snow is piling up all around the car. Are you coming?

BREAD

Bread rising! The intoxicating smell of yeast. And bread fresh from the oven. Someone loves me and has left warm bread. When bread is broken the life hidden within presents itself. A thousand little holes: windows open for the first time. In one booth near the window four old women are drinking tea. They are dressed in old-fashioned clothes, layer on layer, suits and furs, jewelry handed down for generations. One woman names the year of her mother's birth, and another the day her husband died; his clothes still hang in the closet. They talk calmly, quietly, the spring sunlight coming through the glass to touch the backs of their hands . . . . Sit down. Share this bread. As we talk you can explain the ordinary things. I will play some music for you that isn't mine.

A PHOTOGRAPH

She's been dead fifty years now. This photo was taken in 1902, just a girl, clowning for the camera. But when a baby is born in the family someone says, "See it has her eyes, her nose." And it's true. The argument continues. "I'm a farmer," I say, "a business man. I can't be wasting time in town, hanging out at the cafe, drinking coffee." It's spring and the roads are impassable. I stand in the barnyard, knee deep in mud, dumbfounded, surrounded by insolent chickens. She says "I never want to leave here." At night she whispers "You have never loved me. You think only of yourself. You won't be allowed to enter the promised land." Then she giggles and pokes me in the ribs. "The children are asleep now" she says.

WALKING THROUGH A WALL

Unlike flying or astral projection, walking through walls is
a totally earth-related craft, but a lot more interesting than
pot making or driftwood lamps. I got started at a picnic up
in Bowstring in the northern part of the state. A fellow
walked through a brick wall right there in the park. I said
"Say, I want to try that." Stone walls are best, then brick
and wood. Wooden walls with fiberglass insulation and
steel doors aren't so good. They won't hurt you. If your
wall walking is done properly, both you and the wall are
left intact. It is just that they aren't pleasant somehow. The
worst things are wire fences, maybe it's the molecular
structure of the alloy or just the amount of give in a fence, I
don't know, but I've torn my jacket and lost my hat in a lot
of fences. The best approach to a wall is, first, two hands
placed flat against the surface; it's a matter of concentration
and just the right pressure. You will feel the dry, cool inner
wall with your fingers, then there is a moment of total
darkness before you step through on the other side.

Louis Jenkins was born and raised in Oklahoma and attended Wichita State University in Witchita, Kansas. His poetry has been published in a number of magazines, including *American Poetry Review, Ironwood, Poetry East, Paris Review* and *Virginia Quarterly Review*, and included in several anthologies. In addition he has published three chapbooks and was awarded a Bush Foundation Fellowship for poetry in 1979 and again in 1984. Mr. Jenkins, who is married and has one son, has lived in Duluth, Minnesota since 1971.